SEASONS of
GROWTH

SEASONS OF GROWTH

A JOURNAL FOR WELL-BEING INSPIRED BY TREES

MARCUS BRIDGEWATER

HARPERONE

An Imprint of HarperCollins*Publishers*

FIRST EDITION

Designed by Elina Cohen
Tree art © feipco and spot art © TWINS DESIGN STUDIO / Shutterstock

Library of Congress Cataloging-in-Publication Data has been applied for.

ISBN 978-0-06-332118-2

24 25 26 27 28 LBC 5 4 3 2 1

TABLE OF CONTENTS

AN INVITATION TO GROW

Greetings and welcome to this guided journal! I created this resource to help you begin journaling or learn to journal in new ways. Journaling is the practice of taking our thoughts from pen to paper with the intention of finding clarity, organizing the mind, and learning about ourselves. This practice changed my life by providing me with an outlet when I felt trapped, confused, depressed, and unmotivated. It was also there to commemorate moments of joy and celebration, and continues to do so today. I believe it can do the same for others.

In this journal, we will think of ourselves as trees growing through the different seasons, with each season representing a different combination of elements that yields unique challenges, experiences, and opportunities for learning. This will remind us that although growth requires energy and effort, it shouldn't be complicated, and when it is, it is because of our mindset, circumstances, or external pressures. Our journal will be a log of lessons we learn from our experiences, similar to the rings of a tree that mark every year of growth.

We have more in common with trees than we may think. Just as a tree has leaves, a trunk, and roots, we have a mind, body, and spirit. As we think of ourselves as trees, we will assign the major components of trees to ourselves. Our *leaves* correspond to our *mind*, our *trunk* corresponds to our body, and our *roots* correspond to our spirit. A tree's leaves, trunk, and roots adapt to the different seasons, and our mind, body, and spirit must do the same. Most important, just as a tree yearns to grow, so do we.

Like a tree, we want to live in a state of wellness in which we grow to our full potential. This means having peace in our mind, balance in our body, and harmony in our spirit. I define peace as a mental state of calm and clarity. Balance is a physical state of control and stability. Harmony is the spiritual state of being composed, alert, and engaged with both ourselves and the life around us. Similar to the trees in a forest, we do not grow alone. We affect and are affected by *whom* we grow with and *where* we grow—our community and environment. The better we are as individuals, the better we contribute to those around us. Journaling helps us achieve peace, balance, and harmony because it gives us a process to monitor our growth, track our progress, and check in with ourselves.

I frequently champion journaling through my work as a wellness educator, where I reach people through presentations or workshops and by sharing personal-growth insights through plant metaphors on social media as Garden Marcus. Whenever I talk about journaling as a tool for self-discovery and well-being, I'm met with a variety of responses. People often ask: *What should I write about? How do I start?* Others express reluctance to journaling because they're certain it won't serve them, and many people who do try it out give up after a few entries because they don't feel rewarded; without progress or results, why continue?

Writing a single journal entry and expecting your life to turn around is like asking for fruit from a tree you planted yesterday. Growth doesn't just happen—it's a never-ending process, something we should welcome and embrace. It requires work and a commitment to learning, and it's a process that can be observed through the growth of trees. Before a tree can fruit, it needs leaves to collect sunlight for energy, a strong trunk capable of withstanding the elements, established roots capable of absorbing water, and most important, time to grow.

At the most basic level, journaling helps us analyze and reflect on how we spend our time and energy in the world. To me, our hobbies, habits, and routines in particular create the structure of our growth: hobbies are activities we do to feel inspired in our spirit, such as gardening or drawing; habits are settled tendencies we have, like biting our nails or drinking tea, that can be challenging to establish or give up; and routines are processes and procedures we develop to manage the needs of the body and mind, like eating and sleeping. When we journal, we ask ourselves, am I nurturing the hobbies that give me joy, whether that is my evening read of the news on my phone or my Thursday morning yoga class? Are my habits, like my second cup of coffee and biting my nails, serving me? Are my routines, like my wake-up time or afternoon snack, restoring my mind and body? When we journal, we take stock. We look backward in order to look forward. We channel our energy to make the best decisions for our well-being. My goal for you is to create hobbies, habits, and routines that support your growth goals for your mind, body, and spirit throughout the seasons.

Remember that your journal is your own, and there are no rules for how you write, draw, or doodle in it. Whether you write in prose or bullet points, the most important factor is consistency. To get the most out of journaling, I suggest writing regularly. When I'm having a hard time, I might reach for my journal several times a day; when life is less taxing, I aim to journal every day to every few days to check in with myself and what is going on in my life. If you find yourself with "writer's block," the prompts in this book can continue to guide you.

As you complete these prompts, activities, and exercises, I hope you challenge yourself to think deeply about your goals, your growth, how you're tending to yourself, and how you're interacting with those around you. Revisit prompts and see how your answers change. And know that this journal can be started in any season; if it's winter, begin with the winter section. If it's summer, start with summer. Whenever you start, aim to journal through four consecutive seasons so you have a comprehensive understanding of your year and can reflect holistically at the end of it.

Now, let's get started! Here are some introductory prompts to begin, and then you may proceed to the section covering the season you are currently experiencing.

As you answer the prompts, release your inhibitions and judgments. Don't get caught up in how your responses sound or why; just write your truth. Be honest with yourself, and remember that this is a tool to support you.

1. Who are you?

_____

_____

_____

_____

_____

_____

_____

_____

_____

_____

_____

2. What is the current state of your well-being (your mental health, physical fitness, and spiritual awareness)?

_____

_____

_____

_____

_____

_____

_____

_____

_____

_____

_____

_____

3. What are your goals for the coming year?

_____

_____

_____

_____

_____

_____

_____

_____

_____

_____

_____

_____

4. Why is your well-being important?

_____

_____

_____

_____

_____

_____

_____

_____

_____

_____

_____

_____

5. What is your current routine for managing your well-being?

_____

_____

_____

_____

_____

_____

_____

_____

_____

_____

_____

6. What does growth mean to you?

_____

_____

_____

_____

_____

_____

_____

_____

_____

_____

_____

_____

_____

7. Describe your growth over the past year.

_____

_____

_____

_____

_____

_____

_____

_____

_____

_____

_____

_____

8. Do you feel stunted in your growth or supported?

_____

_____

_____

_____

_____

_____

_____

_____

_____

_____

_____

_____

9. What would you like your growth to look like a year from now?

_____
_____
_____
_____
_____
_____
_____
_____
_____
_____
_____
_____
_____
_____
_____
_____
_____
_____
_____
_____
_____
_____
_____
_____
_____
_____
_____

Happy journaling, and here's to the seasons to come.

SUMMER

THE SEASON OF PACING AND KEEPING TEMPO

Summer is the season for continuing the new growth that spring inspired. Our buds transform into leaves, and we focus on strengthening our branches. The green of new stalks and branches turns brown as they become healthy and established, and our leaves soak up bright daylight to give us energy. Hard at work in the summer heat, our roots dig deeper into the ground and reach for moisture to keep us hydrated in the sun.

If spring is a time to awaken from winter's slumber, the summer months are the time to get active and begin reaching for new heights. We feel energized by the sun's rays and the activity of life around us, and motivated to grow with the patterns of nature. However, we can fatigue easily in the brightness and heat, so we need to pace ourselves and keep up our tempo of growth. We don't want to lose the momentum we started in spring, but we also want to avoid burning out before autumn.

Pacing is the practice of managing ourselves, specifically our energy and enthusiasm.

Our inspiration may overtake us with ideas of self-improvement as well as how to share with our community and environment, so we need to apply discipline to ensure our ideas are practical and don't overwhelm us. If this happens, we're likely to procrastinate or stop carrying out our ideas, stalling our growth. Managing our energy and enthusiasm means making a plan and sticking to it, and journaling is a way to do that. We set our goals and write to keep ourselves accountable. It doesn't mean we can't adjust our plan as need be, but we won't lose sight of what's important to us and what we want to achieve.

Keeping tempo is the act of maintaining motivation. Coming up with ideas for our growth and setting goals are the easier parts of the process; implementing them is a greater labor. We may encounter obstacles that force us to reevaluate our direction, and even tempt us to give up, making it seem like we're moving backward instead of forward. In these moments, journaling is an invaluable resource. We can track our mood, our response to challenges, and our approach to finding solutions. This is when it helps to review our goals for growth and our plan to achieve them, and remember that pacing ourselves gives us room to slow down when needed. Managing our energy helps us maintain motivation, and maintaining motivation helps us pace ourselves as we move forward.

Our rhythm, the result of pacing and keeping tempo, does more than support our personal growth. The incremental changes we make are easier for our community and environment to adapt to. Drastic changes can be disruptive to ourselves as well as those around us. What would be the impact of cutting several branches back at once? Would the plants growing near our roots thrive in the increased sunlight or suffer? Are *we* prepared for a great and immediate change? We can't predict the full scope of the impact of a hefty chop, but we can ease ourselves into the process. Trimming over time allows the other plants to adapt and grow with us so we can all grow together.

Let your rhythm help you reach for the sun this season and see what heights you can achieve.

Describe your current state of growth.

_____

_____

_____

_____

_____

_____

_____

_____

_____

_____

_____

1. What are your growth goals this season?

_____

_____

_____

_____

_____

_____

_____

_____

_____

_____

_____

_____

2. Where are you making progress on these goals?

_____
_____
_____
_____
_____
_____
_____
_____
_____
_____
_____
_____

3. Where are you stagnating on these goals?

_____
_____
_____
_____
_____
_____
_____
_____
_____
_____
_____
_____

What are three things you are most looking forward to this summer, and why?

_____
_____
_____
_____
_____
_____
_____
_____
_____
_____
_____
_____

What are three things you are not looking forward to this summer, and why not? How can you grow from these experiences?

_____
_____
_____
_____
_____
_____
_____
_____
_____
_____
_____

On a scale of 1–10, rate your current level of peace, balance, and harmony.

Peace:

Balance:

Harmony:

How does summer affect your motivation to maintain your hobbies, habits, and routines?

_____

_____

_____

_____

_____

_____

_____

_____

_____

_____

_____

_____

_____

_____

_____

_____

_____

The fruit we produce in the summer represents seasons of growth accumulating into something we can share. Ask yourself:

1. What is your fruit? (Is it work, school, a craft, or something else?)

_____
_____
_____
_____
_____
_____
_____

2. Why is this your fruit?

_____
_____
_____
_____
_____

3. Who do you grow this fruit for?

_____
_____
_____
_____
_____
_____

What is your favorite summer memory, and what
stage of growth were you in—seedling, sapling, or
mature tree?

_____

_____

_____

_____

_____

_____

_____

_____

_____

At the height of the summer heat, leaves may
shrivel and go limp to conserve a tree's energy.
Similarly, in the summer of life we are often most
active and energized, though this can make us
grow weary. What is impacting your energy, and
how are you maintaining your momentum?

_____

_____

_____

_____

_____

_____

_____

_____

_____

STRETCH LIKE A TREE EXERCISE

The days are long and the sun is bright—it's the season for high energy. Stand up and take a deep breath as you reach your hands above your head and toward the sky, stretching your body as much as you can and standing on your toes if able. Feel your energy move from your feet to your hands, and stretch out your fingers. Hold the position for a moment, then exhale as you lower your arms and relax your body.

FOR EVERY BRANCH AND LEAF WE SEE ABOVEGROUND, A TREE IS STEADILY EXPANDING ITS ROOTS IN THE SOIL. THIS CREATES A STEADY PACE OF GROWTH, ONE THAT SHOULD NOT BE RUSHED.

1. Is something in your life asking you to move faster than you can?

_____

_____

_____

_____

_____

_____

_____

_____

_____

_____

2. What can you do to slow down?

_____

_____

_____

_____

_____

_____

_____

_____

_____

_____

WHEN THE SUN'S HEAT IS SEEMINGLY INESCAPABLE, WE CAN
FIND COOL, SHADED RELIEF UNDER THE CANOPY OF A TRUSTED
TREE.

1. How easy or difficult is it for you to ask for support?

_____

_____

_____

_____

_____

_____

_____

_____

_____

_____

2. Who asks for your help when problems develop?

_____

_____

_____

_____

_____

_____

_____

_____

_____

_____

3. How do you keep your leaves (your mind) healthy so you can provide shade for others?

_____

_____

_____

_____

_____

_____

_____

_____

_____

_____

A SUMMER THUNDERSTORM BRINGS WINDS, RAIN, AND FLUCTUATING TEMPERATURES. IN SEARCH OF SAFETY, MAMMALS, INSECTS, AND BEINGS OF ALL KINDS MAY TAKE REFUGE IN A SINGLE TREE.

1. Do those in your community respond to adversity individually or as a community?

_____

_____

_____

_____

_____

_____

_____

_____

_____

2. Is your community's response effective? If not, how could it be improved?

_____

_____

_____

_____

_____

_____

_____

_____

_____

_____

THE FRUIT THAT GROWS FROM THE BRANCHES OF A TREE IS LIKE THE THOUGHTS AND EXPERIENCES WE COLLECT EVERY DAY. IT CAN CAUSE OUR BRANCHES TO SNAP AND BREAK IF THE WEIGHT BECOMES MORE THAN WE CAN HANDLE.

1. Does it feel like your branches are getting too heavy?

_____

_____

_____

_____

_____

_____

_____

_____

2. How can you unload the weight of your fruit to protect your branches?

_____

_____

_____

_____

_____

_____

_____

_____

_____

_____

What are two things you do _every day_ to keep tempo? What are two things you do _weekly_ to keep tempo? How do these things help you?

_____

_____

_____

_____

_____

_____

_____

_____

_____

_____

_____

_____

Summer is the season of momentum. Describe what that means for you and your growth right now.

_____

_____

_____

_____

_____

_____

_____

_____

_____

IN THE RAINY SEASON OF A TROPICAL SUMMER, A TREE CAN FACE DAILY STORMS THAT VARY IN THE AMOUNT OF RAIN, LIGHTNING, AND WIND THEY BRING.

1. What was the hardest storm, in all of the summers you have experienced, for you to endure? Describe when it happened and how long it lasted.

_____

_____

_____

_____

_____

_____

_____

_____

_____

_____

2. What were the main challenges you experienced?

_____

_____

_____

_____

_____

_____

_____

_____

_____

_____

_____

3. How did you weather the storm?

_____

_____

_____

_____

_____

_____

_____

_____

_____

_____

_____

_____

NOT EVERY TREE WILL EXPERIENCE THE SAME LEVEL OF
DOWNPOUR FROM A STORM. SOME MAY FACE LIGHTNING
STRIKES, AND OTHERS MAY EMERGE UNSCATHED.

1. What recent challenge have you faced that many others have faced as well?

_____

_____

_____

_____

_____

_____

_____

_____

_____

2. How was your experience different from others going through this experience?

_____

_____

_____

_____

_____

_____

_____

_____

_____

When the "stormy season" has passed, describe
your process of healing from the recent rain.

_____

_____

_____

_____

_____

_____

_____

_____

_____

_____

_____

If you weathered the storms of this summer a year
from now:

1. How would you prepare your leaves?

_____

_____

_____

_____

_____

_____

_____

_____

2. How would you support your trunk?

_____

_____

_____

_____

_____

_____

3. How would you protect your roots?

_____

_____

_____

_____

_____

_____

In what ways do you thrive in summer?

_____

_____

_____

_____

_____

_____

_____

SOME TREES BEGIN FRUITING IN SPRING, AND OTHERS IN LATE
SUMMER. THERE ARE MANY REASONS WHY, RANGING FROM
CLIMATE FACTORS TO THE TREES' UNIQUE GROWTH PATTERNS.
HOWEVER, IT CAN BE DIFFICULT TO WITNESS FRUIT ON ANOTHER
TREE WHEN WE HAVE NOT YET BEGUN TO FLOWER.

1. Do you compare yourself to others?

_____

_____

_____

_____

_____

_____

_____

_____

2. If so, in what ways?

_____

_____

_____

_____

_____

_____

_____

_____

_____

_____

3. Why do you make these comparisons?

_____
_____
_____
_____
_____
_____
_____
_____
_____
_____
_____
_____

4. How do you remind yourself to focus on your own progress when distracted by the progress of others?

_____
_____
_____
_____
_____
_____
_____
_____
_____
_____
_____

SUMMER BREATHING EXERCISE

Center yourself and improve your clarity with this breathing exercise. This can be done standing, sitting, or lying down.

Close your eyes, and picture your entire body. Imagine the air around you moving into your body, circulating, and leaving you. Visualize yourself becoming stronger and calmer with each circulation.

Slowly take a deep breath, drawing in as much air as you can until your lungs are full. When you're at your air capacity, exhale, trying to make your exhale longer than your inhale.

This exercise brings energy, promotes calmness, and provides clarity—especially in moments of challenge.

Describe the environment you write this entry from. How does it contribute to your growth?

_____

_____

_____

_____

_____

_____

_____

_____

_____

_____

_____

We all respond to the summer sun differently. Some of us wholly embrace it for growth, and others do well with some sunlight or just a little. It's time to check in with your _needs_:

1. What is your sunlight, and are you getting enough of it? Too much?

_____

_____

_____

_____

_____

_____

_____

2. Where does your sunlight come from?

_____

_____

_____

_____

_____

_____

_____

_____

_____

POSITIVE AND NEGATIVE THOUGHTS HAVE PROFOUND IMPACTS ON OUR POTENTIAL FOR GROWTH. GROWING WITH POSITIVITY MEANS GROWING WITHOUT LIMITATIONS AND HAVING THE COURAGE TO STRETCH OUR BRANCHES IN ANY DIRECTION. GROWING WITH NEGATIVITY MEANS CONFINING OUR GROWTH TO A COUPLE OF PLACES THAT FEEL SAFE AND SECURE.

1. Are you leading your growth with positivity or negativity?

_____

_____

_____

_____

_____

_____

_____

_____

_____

2. What are two ways your growth is impacted as a result?

_____
_____
_____
_____
_____
_____
_____
_____
_____
_____

3. How are you affected by negativity?

_____
_____
_____
_____
_____
_____
_____
_____
_____
_____

4. When do you feel the most positive?

_____

_____

_____

_____

_____

_____

_____

_____

_____

_____

Describe the current state of your leaves. Are they strong or shriveled? Vibrant or dull?

_____

_____

_____

_____

_____

_____

_____

_____

_____

_____

_____

A tree's roots need enough access to water to withstand the evaporation that happens in the hot summer sun. What water source supports your spirit in times of challenge?

_____

_____

_____

_____

_____

_____

_____

_____

_____

_____

Describe the progress you have made on your growth goals since the season began.

_____

_____

_____

_____

_____

_____

_____

_____

_____

_____

_____

ACTIVITY: BE PRESENT IN THE SUMMER

Distractions are everywhere in our modern age, and they can keep us from focusing on our wellness and growth. We can manage these distractions by making time to actively be present and deepen our connection with ourselves.

One way to do this is by stimulating our senses. It's time to get outside! Use the following checklist to find ways to engage your senses. As you stop to pay attention to the smells, sights, tastes, feelings, and sounds, think about the sensations you experience and how they affect you.

Smell a flower you find growing outside
(but make sure it isn't poisonous!).

Listen to the sounds of nature.

Taste fresh local produce.

Feel the sun on your skin.

See a tree moving in the wind.

Each sensory experience is an opportunity to realign your mind, body, and spirit. Use them to bring yourself to the present moment so your mind is conscious of your body's response, and your spirit is connecting you to your surroundings.

TREE TRUNKS REPRESENT STRENGTH AND BALANCE. IT TAKES
CONSIDERABLE POWER, LIKE LIGHTNING OR AN AXE, TO DAMAGE
THE TRUNK OF A MATURE TREE.

1. What does strength in your body mean to you?

_____

_____

_____

_____

_____

_____

_____

_____

_____

2. How do you promote strength and balance in your body?

_____

_____

_____

_____

_____

_____

_____

_____

_____

_____

_____

SOME TREES ARE KNOWN TO LIVE FOR THOUSANDS OF YEARS,
SURVIVING CENTURIES WHILE OTHER SPECIES LIVE AND PASS
AWAY. THEY SYMBOLIZE STABILITY.

1. Who is a symbol of stability in your life?

_____

_____

_____

_____

_____

_____

_____

_____

_____

_____

2. What do you do to honor those who are symbols of stability in your life?

_____

_____

_____

_____

_____

_____

_____

_____

_____

_____

3. How are you a symbol for stability for others?

_____

_____

_____

_____

_____

_____

_____

_____

_____

_____

_____

_____

Early morning to late night, leaves turn summer sunlight into energy for growth. Considering your leaves, trunk, and roots:

1. Do you prioritize any one part of you (mind, body, spirit) over the others for your growth?

_____

_____

_____

_____

_____

_____

_____

_____

2. What part of you do you struggle most to direct energy into?

_____

_____

_____

_____

_____

_____

_____

_____

3. Do you evenly distribute your energy?

_____

_____

_____

_____

_____

_____

_____

4. Are you neglecting part of yourself?

_____

_____

_____

_____

_____

_____

_____

5. Could you distribute your energy differently for better growth?

_____

_____

_____

_____

_____

_____

_____

_____

_____

Our growth can take different forms. Sometimes we grow out great new branches from the top of our trunk, and sometimes growth comes in smaller shoots from our roots. How are you inspired to grow right now?

_____

_____

_____

_____

_____

_____

_____

_____

_____

_____

_____

_____

IN A DROUGHT, WE MAY STALL NEW GROWTH TO FOCUS ON
SURVIVAL AS OUR ROOTS SEARCH FOR WATER IN THE DRY
GROUND.

1. Are you experiencing a "drought"—relationship problems—with somebody close to you?

_____

_____

_____

_____

_____

_____

_____

_____

_____

2. What can you do to address the problems?

_____

_____

_____

_____

_____

_____

_____

_____

_____

_____

3. How will addressing the problems promote progress in your life/lives?

_____

_____

_____

_____

_____

_____

_____

_____

_____

_____

_____

_____

Reflect on your growth this season:

1. What has changed in your well-being since the summer began?

_____

_____

_____

_____

_____

_____

_____

_____

_____

2. Describe the state of your leaves, trunk, and roots.

_____

_____

_____

_____

_____

_____

_____

_____

_____

_____

3. Do you feel vibrant? If not, what can be done now to prepare for improved growth in the next season?

_____

_____

_____

_____

_____

_____

_____

_____

_____

_____

4. What is the most valuable lesson you learned this summer?

_____

_____

_____

_____

_____

_____

_____

_____

_____

_____

_____

5. What brought you the most joy this summer?

_____

_____

_____

_____

_____

_____

_____

_____

_____

_____

_____

6. What accomplishment of the summer are you most proud of?

FALL

THE SEASON OF TRANSITION, SHARING, AND GRATITUDE

Fall is the season when new growth slows and we move toward rest. We begin storing our energy rather than expending it on outward growth. Our leaves fall to the ground, where they create a blanket that keeps our roots warm when temperatures drop. Letting go of old growth allows our trunk and branches to focus internally, and our roots simultaneously ease their expansion underground. Animals start creating the nests that will protect them from the tough elements, looking to us for shelter and support, and we give back to our community and environment.

Before our leaves make their way down, they transition in color from greens to yellows, reds, oranges, and browns. Our leaves may change colors at different rates, some morphing quickly and others taking time. This represents the ways our varying experiences affect us; we hold on to some tighter than others, but all have the potential to nourish us. In letting our leaves fall, we separate ourselves from our previous experiences and allow ourselves to think about them objectively. This is the process of transitioning from heightened activity to a slower pace, and it helps us grow in the final seasons of the year.

Just as leaves on the ground nurture more beings than the one tree they fell from, we can share what we learn from this seasonal transition to better our community along with ourselves. When we feel as though we don't have anything to offer or share, we may cut ourselves off from others. But if we are consistent in maintaining our well-being and fostering our growth, we will always have something to share that others can benefit from. Our contributions may be knowledge from our unique experiences or what we've learned about how to support growth. Let's not underestimate the impact of sharing our lessons, words of encouragement, and general kindness with others.

Sharing with others and being shared with promotes gratitude, something that is critical to maintaining a positive mindset. Gratitude is the practice of honoring our experiences and what we have. The more we apply it, the easier it is to draw upon our positivity. Our mindset influences how we approach our experiences, and doing so with positivity keeps us focused on growth— particularly when we may be inclined toward negativity. For many, saying goodbye to the long days of summer and greeting the darker days of fall brings a seasonal malaise, and a positive mindset is harder to maintain. This is the time to strengthen our constitution of positivity so we can complete one cycle of growth with vitality and prepare for the one to come.

Let go of old growth and lean into the possibilities the season has to offer.

Describe your current state of growth.

_____

_____

_____

_____

_____

_____

_____

_____

_____

_____

_____

1. What are your growth goals this season?

_____

_____

_____

_____

_____

_____

_____

_____

_____

_____

_____

2. Where are you making progress on these goals?

_____

_____

_____

_____

_____

_____

_____

_____

_____

_____

_____

3. Where are you stagnating on these goals?

_____

_____

_____

_____

_____

_____

_____

_____

_____

_____

_____

_____

What are three things you are most looking forward to this fall, and why?

_____

_____

_____

_____

_____

_____

What are three things you are not looking forward to this fall, and why not? How can you grow from these experiences?

_____

_____

_____

_____

_____

_____

On a scale of 1–10, rate your current level of peace, balance, and harmony.

Peace:

Balance:

Harmony:

Like the leaves that change color and fall from our trees, we too must let go of old growth to prepare for the new. What negative habit will you let go of, and what will you replace it with?

_____

_____

_____

_____

_____

_____

_____

_____

_____

THE TRANSITION OF SUMMER TO FALL AFFECTS US ALL DIFFERENTLY.

1. Where do you feel it the most: your leaves, trunk, or roots?

_____

_____

_____

_____

_____

_____

_____

_____

_____

_____

2. What does the transition mean for your mind, body, and spirit?

_____

_____

_____

_____

_____

_____

_____

_____

_____

_____

Describe your relationship to gratitude. How do you incorporate it into your life?

_____

_____

_____

_____

_____

_____

_____

_____

_____

_____

_____

FALL GROUNDING EXERCISE

A tree's power to grow comes from above and below: the sunlight from the sky that is absorbed by its leaves, as well as the nutrients and water that are collected by its roots in the ground.

We, too, can gather energy from the soil through grounding, the act of connecting with the planet through direct skin-to-earth contact. The earth is like a giant battery; it constantly emits electrical energy. This energy recharges our bodies, and we can enjoy it by putting our feet on the ground.

Find a patch of earth. It doesn't matter if it's your backyard or the grass in the park, but make sure it's free of broken glass or harmful debris before removing your shoes. Ideally, this patch of earth will also be free of chemicals (such as lawn treatment or herbicides) that are known to have toxic properties.

Remove your shoes and place your feet on the ground. This does not have to be done standing—I helped my elderly grandmother ground herself while she sat on the seat of her walker. As long as your bare feet are on the ground, you're grounding!

With your feet on the ground, close your eyes. Focus on the feeling of earth beneath your feet. Consider the texture, temperature, and anything else you notice. Imagine sending your roots down deep into the ground, where they draw nutrients from the ground, and feel them reenergize you and give you strength.

What is the most recent thing (such as a material item, your time, your insight) that you shared with someone? What resulted from the exchange? Who did you share it with, and why?

_____

_____

_____

_____

_____

_____

_____

_____

_____

Parting with leaves of the previous seasons challenges us to confront the past. How do you feel about this process? Are you eager to prepare for new growth or reluctant to begin the process?

_____

_____

_____

_____

_____

_____

_____

_____

The routines of our responsibilities (work, school, etc.) may remain the same in the summer and fall despite the changes in weather and sun patterns. During this transition of longer to shorter days:

1. What do you notice about your productivity?

_____

_____

_____

_____

_____

_____

_____

_____

2. What do you notice about your motivation?

_____

_____

_____

_____

_____

_____

_____

_____

_____

_____

_____

_____

IT'S HEALTHFUL TO BE AWARE OF CHANGES IN OUR BODY, SUCH AS OUR LEAFY BRANCHES CHANGING FROM LUSCIOUS TO BARE.

1. What are three changes you have noticed in your body recently?

_____

_____

_____

_____

_____

_____

_____

_____

_____

_____

2. Are these changes signs of growth? How so?

_____

_____

_____

_____

_____

_____

_____

_____

_____

3. If the changes are signs of decline, how can you address them to support your well-being?

_____

_____

_____

_____

_____

_____

_____

_____

_____

_____

_____

What is a lesson you learned this season that you think others would benefit from, and why?

_____

_____

_____

_____

_____

_____

_____

_____

_____

_____

_____

How does your trunk feel today?

_____

_____

_____

_____

_____

_____

_____

_____

_____

_____

_____

1. Do you feel balanced in your body?

_____

_____

_____

_____

_____

_____

_____

_____

_____

_____

_____

2. If not, what can you do to improve your sense of balance?

_____

_____

_____

_____

_____

_____

_____

_____

_____

_____

_____

The changes in a tree's growth pattern are provoked by changes in weather and sunlight. Is anything provoking you to make changes in your hobbies, habits, and routines right now?

_____

_____

_____

_____

_____

_____

_____

_____

_____

_____

_____

_____

1. How is your community contributing to your growth this season?

_____

_____

_____

_____

_____

_____

_____

_____

_____

_____

2. What are the impacts of their contributions?

_____

_____

_____

_____

_____

_____

_____

_____

_____

_____

_____

THERE IS STRENGTH IN ALLOWING OURSELVES TO PART WITH
THE GROWTH OF THE PREVIOUS SEASON AND GIVE OURSELVES
SPACE TO WELCOME THE NEW.

1. Where do you pull your strength from in the time of transition?

_____

_____

_____

_____

_____

_____

_____

_____

_____

_____

2. What does this strength mean to you?

_____

_____

_____

_____

_____

_____

_____

_____

_____

3. What does this strength feel like to you?

_____

_____

_____

_____

_____

_____

_____

_____

_____

_____

_____

Although our aboveground growth begins to stall in fall, the season gives our roots a chance to continue establishing themselves in the soil. How are you using the season to deepen your connection to your community?

_____

_____

_____

_____

_____

_____

_____

_____

_____

_____

FALL BREATHING EXERCISE

Breathing is a tool to use when we are transitioning between tasks, emotions, and moods. This exercise promotes stability in these moments of change. By controlling our breath, we align the mind and body, and elevate our state of self-awareness.

Breathe in for three seconds.

Hold that breath for five seconds.

Breathe out for six seconds.

Repeat the exercise three times.

Think of each three-five-six cycle as a rep. Two reps become a set. Start with one rep and work up to a set, with the goal of doing three sets at a time comfortably.

Consider the transition from summer to fall:

1. What has been the most challenging for you?

_____

_____

_____

_____

_____

_____

_____

_____

_____

_____

_____

2. What has been the easiest?

_____

_____

_____

_____

_____

_____

_____

_____

_____

_____

_____

3. What were you ready to move on from?

4. What did/do you want to hold on to?

A TREE HAS TO PRACTICE ADAPTING IN EACH SEASON. IN FALL, ADAPTATION CAN INCLUDE SAYING GOODBYE TO THE FINAL BLOOMS OF SUMMER. IT CAN BE HARD TO EMBRACE THESE SEASONAL CHANGES, BUT IT'S ESSENTIAL FOR GROWTH.

1. What changes are you currently adapting to?

_____

_____

_____

_____

_____

_____

_____

_____

2. How are you adapting so you can grow through these changes?

_____

_____

_____

_____

_____

_____

_____

_____

_____

What skill of yours is appreciated by your community?

_____

_____

_____

_____

_____

_____

_____

_____

_____

_____

_____

1. How do you share this skill?

_____

_____

_____

_____

_____

_____

_____

_____

_____

_____

_____

_____

2. Does this skill come naturally to you?

_____

_____

_____

_____

_____

_____

_____

_____

_____

_____

_____

_____

3. Is this skill something you have practiced over time?

_____

_____

_____

_____

_____

_____

_____

_____

_____

_____

_____

The way leaves fall from branches and nurture
roots parallels how the lessons we learn become a
part of us, strengthening our foundation for years
to come. What lesson did you learn last year that
you frequently think about still?

_____

_____

_____

_____

_____

_____

_____

_____

_____

_____

How does your body respond to the energetic
deceleration of the season?

_____

_____

_____

_____

_____

_____

_____

_____

_____

How easy or difficult is it for you to make time for your mental health this season? Is the time you are allocating to your mind enough?

_____

_____

_____

_____

_____

_____

_____

_____

_____

_____

PRUNING IS THE ACT OF CUTTING BACK A TREE'S BRANCHES, AND IT CAN SUPPORT IMPROVED GROWTH. HOWEVER, PRUNING IN THE FALL CAN LEAVE A TREE VULNERABLE TO THE FROST OF WINTER, LEADING TO DAMAGE AND STIFLED GROWTH.

1. Did you move too quickly on a goal or project this season? What happened?

_____

_____

_____

_____

_____

_____

_____

_____

2. How would you approach the process in the future?

_____

_____

_____

_____

_____

_____

_____

_____

_____

_____

_____

FALL, WITH ITS CRISP AIR AND COLORFUL LANDSCAPE, BRINGS
CHANGES TO OUR NEEDS AND INSPIRATION.

1. What are three of your main needs this time of year?

_____

_____

_____

_____

_____

_____

_____

_____

_____

2. Are you meeting your needs? What does that mean for you?

_____

_____

_____

_____

_____

_____

_____

_____

_____

_____

_____

_____

3. What inspires you this time of year?

_____

_____

_____

_____

_____

_____

_____

_____

_____

_____

_____

_____

4. What do you do with that inspiration?

_____
_____
_____
_____
_____
_____
_____
_____
_____
_____
_____
_____

5. If you feel uninspired, why is that?

_____
_____
_____
_____
_____
_____
_____
_____
_____
_____
_____
_____

Describe the environment you write this entry from and how it contributes to your growth.

_____

_____

_____

_____

_____

_____

_____

_____

_____

_____

_____

_____

_____

_____

_____

_____

_____

_____

_____

_____

_____

_____

_____

_____

_____

FALL SHARING ACTIVITY

To celebrate this season of sharing, let's share some positivity with others!

Get a standard piece of paper and cut it into six sections, or acquire six small pieces of paper. Use each paper to write an affirmation, a lesson you learned this season, something you saw recently that made you smile, or some other uplifting thing that comes to mind. Keep the notes short, using the space you have. Share the notes with friends, family, or others who could enjoy your gift. Reflect on their responses as well as the connection between sharing and community.

In this season, the sun sets sooner and shortens the long days we knew in summer. How will this difference affect your leaves, trunk, and roots individually, as well as your well-being holistically?

_____

_____

_____

_____

_____

_____

_____

_____

_____

What are two ways you slow down and begin storing your energy instead of expending it?

_____

_____

_____

_____

_____

_____

_____

_____

_____

_____

What is something you have to share with others this fall that you did not have last fall? How did you come to attain it, and how do you share it?

_____

_____

_____

_____

_____

_____

_____

_____

_____

_____

Reflect on your growth this season:

1. What has changed in your well-being since the fall began?

_____

_____

_____

_____

_____

_____

_____

_____

_____

_____

2. Describe the state of your leaves, trunk, and roots.

_____

_____

_____

_____

_____

_____

_____

_____

_____

_____

_____

_____

3. Do you feel nourished? If not, what can be done now to prepare for improved growth in the next season?

_____

_____

_____

_____

_____

_____

_____

_____

_____

_____

_____

_____

4. What is the most valuable lesson you learned this fall?

_____
_____
_____
_____
_____
_____
_____
_____
_____
_____
_____
_____
_____

5. What brought you the most joy this fall?

_____
_____
_____
_____
_____
_____
_____
_____
_____
_____
_____
_____

6. What accomplishment of the fall are you most proud of?

WINTER

THE SEASON TO REST, REFLECT, AND PREPARE

Winter marks the end of a cycle, seasons of growth coming to completion. Our roots lie dormant and conserve energy to maintain our health and longevity. Strong and resilient in winter's chill, our branches and trunk withstand the challenge of the frigid conditions in anticipation of new leaves in spring. The layer of our fallen leaves on the ground continues to keep our roots warm as well as nurture them with nutrients and minerals, supporting and protecting us through the season.

The shorter days and longer nights encourage us to rest, reflect, and prepare for new growth to come when the sun returns. We rest so we can stabilize and recharge our energy. Once we're rested, we can productively reflect on our experiences and focus on the lessons we learned in the previous seasons. We can then use this reflection to prepare for the next phase of our growth with a clear direction.

Proper rest serves the mind, body, *and* spirit, not just one or two parts of ourselves. It means giving all three key facets of our being the chance to recuperate. Resting can be both passive and active, and I recommend both to fully restore the self. A night's sleep or a long, much-needed nap are examples of passive rest, while active rest includes meditation and stretching that stimulates the mind, body, and spirit. There are times when we benefit from resting the mind, body, or spirit individually, but we shouldn't neglect addressing them together.

The clarity provided by rest enables us to reflect on our experiences with objectivity and thoughtfulness. The goal of reflection is to consider our choices and actions in the previous seasons and learn the lessons that will guide us in times to come. These lessons come from experiences positive and negative, and reflection is incomplete without considering both. This journal is a great resource to support your reflection and hopefully will inspire you to revisit these prompts and continue journaling in the future. Talking with a trusted friend is another quality way to reflect on your experiences.

Equipped with solid rest and reflection, we are ready to prepare for growth. We create a plan for what we want our growth to look like and how we will achieve it. We think of our goals, where we want to be a year from now, and what we will do to make this vision our reality. As we prepare, we may be filled with inspiration and motivation, and this is a beautiful place to be. Let's remember there's no need to rush, and we have several seasons of growth ahead.

Embrace the season fully and grow stronger from your perseverance through its chill.

Describe your current state of growth.

_____

_____

_____

_____

_____

_____

_____

_____

_____

_____

_____

_____

_____

1. Do you have goals for your well-being?

_____

_____

_____

_____

_____

_____

_____

_____

_____

_____

_____

_____

2. Where are you making progress on these goals?

_____

_____

_____

_____

_____

_____

_____

_____

_____

_____

_____

_____

3. Where are you stagnating on these goals?

_____

_____

_____

_____

_____

_____

_____

_____

_____

_____

_____

_____

_____

What are three things you are looking forward to this winter, and why?

_____

_____

_____

_____

_____

_____

_____

_____

_____

_____

What are three things you are not looking forward to this winter, and why not? How can you grow from these experiences?

_____

_____

_____

_____

_____

_____

_____

_____

_____

_____

On a scale of 1–10, rate your current level of peace, balance, and harmony.

Peace:

Balance:

Harmony:

In the darkness and chill of winter:

1. Where do you draw your energy from?

_____

_____

_____

_____

_____

_____

_____

_____

_____

_____

_____

_____

_____

_____

2. What gives you energy when you feel as though you have none?

_____

_____

_____

_____

_____

_____

_____

_____

_____

_____

As the darkness and chill grow:

1. How does your energy change throughout the day?

_____

_____

_____

_____

_____

_____

_____

_____

_____

_____

2. What are three words to describe your energy five hours ago?

_____

_____

_____

_____

_____

_____

_____

_____

_____

_____

_____

_____

3. What are three words to describe your energy now?

_____

_____

_____

_____

_____

_____

_____

_____

_____

_____

_____

_____

SQUIRRELS ARE KNOWN TO LIVE IN TREES OVER THE WINTER,
OFTEN IN NESTS BUILT ON BRANCHES OR IN A WARM NOOK
WITHIN A TRUNK. OFTEN IN THE DARK OR HARD SEASONS OF
LIFE, WE MUST SUPPORT OTHERS AROUND US—THE SQUIRRELS
TO OUR TREES.

1. Are you supporting anyone right now?

_____

_____

_____

_____

_____

_____

_____

_____

_____

2. Is your support coming from your leaves (your mind) or your trunk (your body)?

_____

_____

_____

_____

_____

_____

_____

_____

_____

3. How are your roots managing the output of energy?

_____

_____

_____

_____

_____

_____

_____

_____

_____

_____

AFTER PROVIDING SHELTER TO THE SQUIRRELS THAT HAVE COME TO US FOR SUPPORT, LET'S THINK ABOUT OUR RELATIONSHIP(S).

1. Is the person or people you're supporting contributing to your well-being?

_____

_____

_____

_____

_____

_____

_____

_____

_____

2. If not, what can you do to foster a reciprocal relationship?

WINTER FREE DRAW ACTIVITY

Let's engage our creativity to promote a state of mental relaxation.

Put your writing utensil to paper and draw a line—straight, curved, it's up to you! Next, do it again and again. Feel free to create a pattern or don't. Your lines can intersect, become shapes, or remain independent. The goal is to follow your inspiration and let your imagination guide you. Rather than aiming to complete a "pretty picture," use this space to lose yourself in the swirls of your pen and creativity. This is a great activity to get our thoughts flowing when we feel uninspired, are confronting a problem and struggling to find a solution, or need to let go of mental tension.

PREPARING FOR THE NEXT CYCLE OF GROWTH INCLUDES
CREATING A PLAN.

1. Where would you like to be a year from now?

_____

_____

_____

_____

_____

_____

_____

_____

_____

_____

_____

2. How will you work toward this vision in the following season?

_____

_____

_____

_____

_____

_____

_____

_____

_____

THINK OF EACH LEAF THAT FELL TO THE GROUND AND WARMS
YOUR ROOTS AS AN EXPERIENCE FROM THE PREVIOUS YEAR.

1. What are three experiences that defined your year?

_____

_____

_____

_____

_____

_____

_____

_____

_____

_____

2. What are three experiences that shaped your growth?

_____

_____

_____

_____

_____

_____

_____

_____

_____

What part of you feels most fatigued right now—your mind, body, or spirit? How can you rest this part of you, and when will you make time for it?

_____

_____

_____

_____

_____

_____

_____

_____

_____

IN THIS SEASON OF REFLECTION, THERE ARE TIMES WHEN WE MAY FOCUS ON MISTAKES OR CHOICES WE WOULD PREFER TO FORGET. IN THESE MOMENTS, WE NEED TO REMIND OURSELVES THAT THE MOST PRODUCTIVE PATH FOR OUR GROWTH, COMMUNITY, AND ENVIRONMENT IS TO LEARN FROM THE EXPERIENCES AND MAKE DIFFERENT CHOICES IN THE FUTURE.

1. Are any of the choices you made in the past year weighing on you?

_____

_____

_____

_____

_____

_____

_____

2. Why did you make the choice(s) you did?

3. Did you anticipate the resulting experience(s)?

4. What about the resulting experience(s) is bothering you?

_____

_____

_____

_____

_____

_____

_____

_____

_____

_____

_____

5. What lesson(s) can you learn from the choice and experience?

_____

_____

_____

_____

_____

_____

_____

_____

_____

_____

_____

_____

Write down two activities in your routine that support your mental well-being.

_____

_____

_____

_____

_____

_____

_____

_____

_____

_____

_____

1. When did these activities become habits?

_____

_____

_____

_____

_____

_____

_____

_____

_____

_____

_____

_____

2. Why did these activities become habits?

_____

_____

_____

_____

_____

_____

_____

_____

_____

_____

_____

_____

3. How has your mental health improved as a result of these habits?

_____

_____

_____

_____

_____

_____

_____

_____

_____

_____

_____

_____

4. If you don't have any, what habits can you begin?

_____

_____

_____

_____

_____

_____

_____

_____

_____

_____

_____

_____

Do you feel like a tree in a forest, surrounded by other trees and protected from the cold winds of winter, or one alone in a field, left to face the chill alone? Why?

_____

_____

_____

_____

_____

_____

_____

_____

_____

_____

IT CAN FEEL AS THOUGH OUR GROWTH IS STAGNATING THIS
SEASON WITHOUT NEW LEAVES OR BRANCHES TO MARK
THE CHANGES WE EXPERIENCE. LET'S REMEMBER WE ARE
STILL GROWING, AND THE SENSE OF STAGNATION CAN BE AN
OPPORTUNITY FOR REST AND PREPARATION.

1. How have you grown in your mental health,
physical fitness, and spiritual awareness this
season?

_____

_____

_____

_____

_____

_____

_____

2. Describe similarities between the growth you're
experiencing now and the growth you experienced
in summer.

_____

_____

_____

_____

_____

_____

_____

_____

3. Describe differences between the growth you're experiencing now and the growth you experienced in spring.

_____
_____
_____
_____
_____
_____
_____
_____
_____
_____

4. Describe commonalities between the growth you're experiencing now and the growth you experienced in fall.

_____
_____
_____
_____
_____
_____
_____
_____
_____
_____

THE SLOW, UNHURRIED PACE OF WINTER MAKES IT THE IDEAL TIME FOR REST AND ENERGY RESTORATION.

1. What does rest look like for you this time of year?

_____

_____

_____

_____

_____

_____

_____

_____

_____

_____

2. How often do you practice passive rest, and how often do you practice active rest?

_____

_____

_____

_____

_____

_____

_____

_____

_____

3. How is your energy affected by the different practices of rest?

_____

_____

_____

_____

_____

_____

_____

_____

_____

_____

_____

_____

4. How much rest, and in which forms, do you need to feel the most energized?

_____

_____

_____

_____

_____

_____

_____

_____

_____

_____

Not everything changes with the seasons—some trees are known to maintain their green leaves through frost and snow. What are two things that benefit your mental health year-round? How do they help you?

_____

_____

_____

_____

_____

_____

_____

_____

We don't stop working in winter, even if it seems as though our growth has slowed. Describe someone in your community who is hardworking. What can you learn from that person?

_____

_____

_____

_____

_____

_____

_____

_____

WINTER BREATHING EXERCISE

1. As part of our winter reflection, let's take a moment to consider our breathing. Set a timer for one minute and prepare to breathe. Start the timer and breathe as you normally do with increased focus. Count how many seconds your inhales and exhales are. Do you hold your breath between the in and out? If so, for how long? Do you breathe through your mouth, nose, or both? Are your breaths shallow or deep?

2. When the timer chimes, write down your observations. What did you learn from the minute? Describe your emotions before, during, and after the minute.

How do you keep your trunk strong during winter?

_____

_____

_____

_____

_____

_____

_____

_____

_____

_____

WE CAN LOSE OUR INSPIRATION AND MOTIVATION TO GROW
WITH LESS SUN ON OUR LEAVES AND DECREASED ACTIVITY OF
LIFE AROUND US. A DEPRESSION UNIQUE TO THE SEASON MAY
CHALLENGE OUR DRIVE TO WORK ON WELL-BEING.

1. Are you having trouble dedicating time to your mind, body, and spirit?

_____

_____

_____

_____

_____

_____

_____

_____

_____

2. Which part are you struggling to work on the most? Why?

_____

_____

_____

_____

_____

_____

_____

_____

_____

_____

_____

3. How is this struggle affecting your sense of wellness?

_____

_____

_____

_____

_____

_____

_____

_____

_____

_____

_____

4. What can you do to overcome the struggle?

_____

_____

_____

_____

_____

_____

_____

_____

_____

_____

_____

_____

What have you learned from your winter reflecting that will help you prepare for the next cycle of growth?

_____

_____

_____

_____

_____

_____

_____

_____

_____

_____

_____

WINTER LETTER ACTIVITY

When ice and snow cover the ground, a tree's roots continue working to survive beneath the soil. Write a letter to someone who reminds you of the protective layer on a tree's roots and who has recently contributed to the well-being of your spirit.

Describe the environment you write this entry from and how it contributes to your growth.

_____

_____

_____

_____

_____

_____

_____

_____

_____

_____

_____

If you could talk to yourself in the previous winter, what would you say and why?

_____

_____

_____

_____

_____

_____

_____

_____

_____

_____

_____

A TREE IN A GENERALLY WARM REGION MAY BE UNPREPARED
FOR THE HARD FREEZE OF AN UNPREDICTABLE WINTER. TO
SURVIVE, THE TREE MUST ADAPT, EVEN IF IT MEANS LOSING ALL
ITS LEAVES AND PUSHING OUT NEW LIFE FROM THE BASE OF ITS
ROOTS, CHANGING ITS DIRECTION OF GROWTH.

1. What situation has challenged you to adapt recently?

_____

_____

_____

_____

_____

_____

_____

_____

_____

2. How did it affect your trunk, leaves, and roots?

_____

_____

_____

_____

_____

_____

_____

_____

_____

3. Did the situation force you to start growing from your roots, or were you able to continue growing new leaves from your branches?

_____

_____

_____

_____

_____

_____

_____

_____

_____

_____

Describe your approach to preparation.

_____

_____

_____

_____

_____

_____

_____

_____

_____

_____

_____

Now ask yourself:

1. What part of the process do you enjoy the most?

_____

_____

_____

_____

_____

_____

_____

_____

_____

_____

2. What part of the process do you enjoy the least?

_____

_____

_____

_____

_____

_____

_____

_____

_____

_____

3. What part of the process is the hardest for you to execute?

_____

_____

_____

_____

_____

_____

_____

_____

_____

_____

4. What part of the process is the easiest for you to execute?

_____

_____

_____

_____

_____

_____

_____

_____

_____

_____

1. Describe your immediate community in three words.

_____

_____

_____

_____

_____

_____

_____

_____

_____

_____

2. Is this your community by choice or circumstance?

_____

_____

_____

_____

_____

_____

_____

_____

_____

_____

_____

3. Do you trust your community to look out for you?

_____

_____

_____

_____

_____

_____

_____

_____

_____

_____

4. Do your interests align with the interests of your community?

_____

_____

_____

_____

_____

_____

_____

_____

_____

_____

5. Does your community support and encourage your growth?

_____
_____
_____
_____
_____
_____
_____
_____
_____
_____
_____

What advice would you share with others preparing for the next cycle of growth?

_____
_____
_____
_____
_____
_____
_____
_____
_____
_____
_____
_____

JUST AS A BITTER FROST CAN CAUSE IRREPARABLE DAMAGE TO A TREE, OUR WELL-BEING IS SUBJECT TO THE HARSHNESS OF THE SEASON.

1. Have you experienced a "frost" recently?

_____

_____

_____

_____

_____

_____

_____

_____

_____

_____

2. Do you anticipate a coming "frost"?

_____

_____

_____

_____

_____

_____

_____

_____

_____

_____

_____

3. Are you prepared for it?

_____

_____

_____

_____

_____

_____

_____

_____

_____

_____

_____

_____

4. What are you doing to prepare?

_____

_____

_____

_____

_____

_____

_____

_____

_____

_____

_____

WINTER REST AND REFLECT EXERCISE

Let's take some time to relax our bodies as we rest and prepare for new growth.

Lie down on your back in a comfortable setting and close your eyes. You might prefer to do this exercise in a dark place. Once you get into position, try not to move or wriggle around. Through this exercise, we will practice deepening our sense of relaxation by addressing our bodies head to toe. Prepare to spend at least ten minutes on the exercise. By the end we will have strengthened the connection of our mind, body, and spirit.

Direct your focus to your head. Is your face relaxed? Are you holding tension in your eyebrows? Anywhere you find tension, let it go.

Move your focus to your neck, shoulders, and then chest. Are you scrunching your shoulders? Has your neck relaxed, or does it feel like it needs to continue supporting your head as if you are standing?

Continue to ask yourself if you are tense or rigid as you bring your focus to your arms, stomach, hips, legs, and toes. Use this time to bring yourself to a state of complete relaxation so every part of you is aligned and rested.

When you reach your toes, release any final tension you identify, and try to lie for at least five additional minutes to enjoy the attention you have given yourself.

Has your growth plan or goals for the coming year changed since the season began?

_____

_____

_____

_____

_____

_____

_____

_____

_____

_____

In the depth of winter, fewer creatures roam to and fro. As we are drawn to the indoors, we may see fewer people and feel lonely. How do you foster community in these times?

_____

_____

_____

_____

_____

_____

_____

_____

_____

_____

Reflect on your growth this season:

1. What has changed in your well-being since the winter began?

_____

_____

_____

_____

_____

_____

_____

_____

2. Describe the state of your leaves, trunk, and roots.

_____

_____

_____

_____

_____

_____

_____

_____

_____

_____

_____

_____

3. Do you feel rested? If not, what can be done now to prepare for improved growth in the next season?

_____

_____

_____

_____

_____

_____

_____

_____

_____

_____

_____

4. What is the most valuable lesson you learned this winter?

_____

_____

_____

_____

_____

_____

_____

_____

_____

_____

_____

_____

5. What brought you the most joy this winter?

_____

_____

_____

_____

_____

_____

_____

_____

_____

_____

_____

6. What accomplishment of the winter are you most proud of?

_____

_____

_____

_____

_____

_____

_____

_____

_____

_____

_____

SPRING

THE SEASON FOR INSPIRATION, MOMENTUM, AND NEW GROWTH

Spring is the season of renewal and restoration. After a season of rest, our roots awaken and eagerly begin to spread beneath the soil. Our branches, more resilient from surviving the harshness of winter, begin to put out buds that will blossom into young green leaves. These leaves turn sunlight into sustenance that provides us with energy to support new growth in our roots, which in turn supports the growth of new leaves. In a beautiful exchange, we establish a rhythm that enables us to grow robustly.

We spent winter resting, reflecting, and preparing so we could enter spring focused and rejuvenated. The warmer temperatures, emerging flowers, and active wildlife are revitalizing after the tough temperament of winter. Spring's warmth and uplifting energy are nature's encouragement for us to be inspired, proactive, and observant so we can harness all the season has to offer. We enter spring refreshed for inspiration, momentum, and new growth.

From winter's preparation comes spring's inspiration and the drive to act on our growth and goals. Spring is a wonderful time for inspiration because we do not have to dig deep into ourselves to find it; we can summon it from nature, from the sprouting seeds and blooming flowers around us. With a vision of peace, balance, and harmony in our well-being, we yearn to try new things to support our wellness. We take the first steps to establishing new hobbies, habits, and routines that we will continue through this year.

Harnessing our inspiration to begin new hobbies, habits, and routines is only one part of the process; to sustain them, we need to establish momentum. This includes readying ourselves for disruptions and obstacles, because they will come and throw us off course if we are not prepared to confront them and adapt. When we're in the early stages of developing our hobbies, habits, and routines, the difficulties we face can threaten our inspiration, and therefore our growth. The stronger our momentum, the easier it will be for us to continue working on our goals regardless of our circumstances.

Embracing nature's inspiration and resilience through our momentum, we will find ourselves in new territory, with new challenges and new experiences. This is new growth, and it is an opportunity to harness our potential. It doesn't mean everything in our lives will fall into place and problems will be a thing of the past. Instead, it means we are aware of what we need to support our mental health, physical fitness, and spiritual awareness as well as how to navigate our experiences while prioritizing our well-being. When difficulties do present themselves, we will be better equipped to manage them and keep growing.

Use the season's energy to fertilize your well-being and unfurl the leaves of your potential.

Describe your current state of growth.

_____

_____

_____

_____

_____

_____

_____

_____

_____

_____

_____

_____

1. Do you have goals for your well-being?

_____

_____

_____

_____

_____

_____

_____

_____

_____

_____

_____

2. Where are you making progress on these goals?

_____

_____

_____

_____

_____

_____

_____

_____

_____

_____

_____

_____

3. Where are you stagnating on these goals?

_____

_____

_____

_____

_____

_____

_____

_____

_____

_____

_____

_____

What are three things you are looking forward to this season, and why?

_____

_____

_____

_____

_____

_____

_____

_____

_____

_____

_____

_____

_____

What are three things you are not looking forward to this spring, and why not? How can you grow from these experiences?

_____

_____

_____

_____

_____

_____

_____

_____

_____

_____

_____

On a scale of 1–10, rate your current level of peace, balance, and harmony.

Peace:

Balance:

Harmony:

BEES AND BUTTERFLIES RETURN TO THEIR VITAL ROLE OF POLLINATING IN THE SPRING, AND OUR ECOSYSTEMS PROSPER AS A RESULT. EACH OF US HAS THE POTENTIAL TO BE A BEE OR BUTTERFLY AND CONTRIBUTE TO THE BETTERMENT OF OUR ENVIRONMENT.

1. Describe your environment this time of year.

_____

_____

_____

_____

_____

_____

_____

_____

_____

_____

_____

_____

2. How are you contributing to the continued success of your environment?

_____

_____

_____

_____

_____

_____

_____

_____

_____

_____

3. Is your environment promoting your growth?

_____

_____

_____

_____

_____

_____

_____

_____

_____

_____

_____

4. How could the state of your environment improve?

_____

_____

_____

_____

_____

_____

_____

_____

_____

_____

_____

What motivates you to support the growth of your leaves and develop new positive habits?

_____

_____

_____

_____

_____

_____

_____

_____

_____

_____

_____

Do you feel prepared for the challenges to come this season? Why or why not?

_____

_____

_____

_____

_____

_____

_____

_____

_____

_____

_____

_____

A TREE'S ROOTS ARE EAGER TO SPREAD AFTER THE WINTER MONTHS OF PATIENCE AND REST.

1. Where are you growing your roots this spring?

_____

_____

_____

_____

_____

_____

_____

_____

_____

2. What does this mean for your well-being and harmony?

_____

_____

_____

_____

_____

_____

_____

_____

_____

_____

_____

What do you want the "new growth" you are fostering now to look like next spring?

_____

_____

_____

_____

_____

_____

_____

_____

_____

_____

_____

What are you doing to create momentum in your hobbies, habits, and routines?

_____

_____

_____

_____

_____

_____

_____

_____

_____

_____

_____

Consider your mobility and flexibility today and a year ago. Is there improvement or decline? What changed, and how will your current state affect you in the long term?

_____

_____

_____

_____

_____

_____

_____

_____

SPRING BREATHING EXERCISE

Balance your rhythm to maintain your momentum with this breathing exercise. We will alternate inhaling and exhaling between mouth and nose to practice different ways of breathing. This exercise especially helps us establish a calmer rhythm when we find ourselves moving faster than we need to.

1. Inhale through your nose for three seconds, and exhale through your mouth for four seconds.

2. Inhale through your mouth for three seconds, and exhale through your nose for four seconds.

3. Repeat steps 1 and 2 once more.

What did you notice about the breathing cycle? How did it affect you?

Are any disruptions or distractions preventing you from establishing a routine for growth? What can be done to maintain or improve your focus?

_____

_____

_____

_____

_____

_____

_____

_____

_____

_____

_____

Spend time, even a few moments, outdoors or looking out a window. What do you see, hear, or smell that inspires you?

_____

_____

_____

_____

_____

_____

_____

_____

_____

THE RAPID GROWTH OF THE LEAVES ON A NEIGHBORING TREE CAN CHANGE OUR ACCESS TO THE SUN. THIS MAY CAUSE US TO CHANGE OUR DIRECTION OF GROWTH AS WE SEARCH FOR SUFFICIENT LIGHT. DESPITE THE OBSTACLE, WE STILL HAVE AGENCY IN OUR PURSUIT OF GROWTH.

1. Do you feel that something is currently challenging your agency?

_____

_____

_____

_____

_____

_____

_____

_____

_____

2. How do you assert agency in your growth?

_____

_____

_____

_____

_____

_____

_____

_____

_____

_____

_____

Describe the environment you write this entry from. How does it contribute to your growth?

_____
_____
_____
_____
_____
_____
_____
_____
_____
_____
_____

THE END OF WINTER PROMPTS MANY BIRDS TO MIGRATE TO NEW HOMES FOR THE WARMER SEASONS. THEY FIND TWIGS AND STICKS TO BUILD NEW NESTS AND SETTLE INTO THE COMFORT OF A TREE.

1. Whom do your branches support?

_____
_____
_____
_____
_____
_____
_____
_____

2. Do the people you support with your branches change with the season?

_____

_____

_____

_____

_____

_____

_____

_____

_____

_____

_____

3. Are your branches strong and resolute, or breaking under the weight of the nests you support?

_____

_____

_____

_____

_____

_____

_____

_____

_____

4. Are the people you support fostering your growth or hindering it?

_____

_____

_____

_____

_____

_____

_____

_____

_____

_____

5. If you're feeling hindered, what can you do to protect yourself and your ability to continue supporting your community?

_____

_____

_____

_____

_____

_____

_____

_____

_____

_____

_____

If you were a tree in bloom right now, what would your flowers look like and why?

_____

_____

_____

_____

_____

_____

_____

_____

_____

_____

_____

_____

_____

_____

_____

_____

_____

_____

_____

_____

_____

_____

_____

_____

_____

_____

_____

SPRING DRAW A PICTURE WITH WORDS ACTIVITY

Let's exercise our imagination with this word picture activity!

Choose five meaningful and uplifting words—for example, smile, upbeat, energetic, grow, cheer.

Use your chosen words to draw a tree. Instead of lines and curves, your words will construct your drawing. Include roots, a trunk, branches, and leaves. Other than that, follow your imagination and creativity.

Our trees will be a symbol of inspiration for us, and we can look back on them when we need some encouragement.

NEW LEAVES ARE GROWING ON YOUR BRANCHES, OR MAYBE
SOMETHING NEW IS BURGEONING FROM YOUR ROOTS.

1. What is your "new growth"?

_____

_____

_____

_____

_____

_____

_____

_____

_____

_____

2. What does the new growth feel like?

_____

_____

_____

_____

_____

_____

_____

_____

_____

_____

3. Do you notice any impacts of the new growth on yourself, your community, or your environment?

_____

_____

_____

_____

_____

_____

_____

_____

_____

_____

_____

SPRING'S SUNLIGHT CAN SATURATE OUR BODIES DEEPLY, WARMING US FROM THE CHILL OF WINTER.

1. When was the last time your body felt truly relaxed and free of tension?

_____

_____

_____

_____

_____

_____

_____

_____

2. Are you currently holding tension in your body? If so, where?

_____

_____

_____

_____

_____

_____

_____

_____

_____

_____

3. What can you do to alleviate it?

_____

_____

_____

_____

_____

_____

_____

_____

_____

_____

Have you started any hobbies, habits, or routines that you don't see yourself continuing into the next season? Why or why not?

_____

_____

_____

_____

_____

_____

_____

_____

_____

_____

_____

PLANTS, INSECTS, AND ANIMALS AWAKEN WITH ENERGY IN THE NEW SUNS OF SPRING.

1. Describe your current level of energy.

_____

_____

_____

_____

_____

_____

_____

_____

_____

2. Is your energy supporting or hindering your hobbies, habits, and routines?

_____

_____

_____

_____

_____

_____

_____

_____

_____

_____

_____

3. Is anything distracting you from your hobbies, habits, and routines?

_____

_____

_____

_____

_____

_____

_____

_____

_____

_____

"Spring showers" bring us the moisture and nutrients we need to grow and flourish. What has nourished you recently?

_____

_____

_____

_____

_____

_____

_____

_____

_____

_____

What are the greatest differences between the state of your mind, body, and spirit in the previous season and this spring?

_____

_____

_____

_____

_____

_____

_____

_____

_____

_____

**What recent obstacle challenged your momentum?
How did you manage the obstacle?**

_____

_____

_____

_____

_____

_____

_____

_____

_____

_____

_____

**The deeper, longer, and more established our roots
are, the more likely they are to intertwine with the
roots of another tree. Who is bringing harmony to
your spirit right now?**

_____

_____

_____

_____

_____

_____

_____

_____

_____

DESPITE THE COUNTLESS DIFFERENCES AMONG THE TREES AROUND THE WORLD, ALL SHARE SOMETHING IN COMMON: INSPIRATION TO GROW.

1. What is inspiring you right now?

_____

_____

_____

_____

_____

_____

_____

_____

_____

2. Who is inspiring you right now?

_____

_____

_____

_____

_____

_____

_____

_____

_____

_____

3. How are you practicing your inspiration?

_____

_____

_____

_____

_____

_____

_____

_____

SPRING'S BLOOMS AND SUNSHINE CAN TEMPT US TO SPEND ALL OUR TIME OUTDOORS, SMELLING FLOWERS AND ENJOYING THE WARMTH. HOWEVER, WE NEED TO BALANCE INDULGENCE WITH MANAGING OUR RESPONSIBILITIES SO WE DON'T DISRUPT OUR GROWTH.

1. Is discipline easy or hard for you to practice?

_____

_____

_____

_____

_____

_____

_____

_____

_____

_____

_____

_____

2. Are you practicing discipline in your hobbies, habits, and routines?

_____

_____

_____

_____

_____

_____

_____

_____

_____

_____

At this point in the previous spring, did you notice any new growth? What was it? How has it manifested in your well-being this spring?

_____

_____

_____

_____

_____

_____

_____

_____

_____

WE FEEL OURSELVES GROWING, STRETCHING OUR BRANCHES
AND REACHING FOR THE SUN, AND THEN THE BRANCH OF A
NEARBY TREE BREAKS, FALLING ON US AND HITTING ONE OF OUR
BRANCHES.

1. Have you experienced a conflict with someone in your community recently?

_____

_____

_____

_____

_____

_____

_____

_____

_____

_____

2. Did/does this conflict hinder your growth?

_____

_____

_____

_____

_____

_____

_____

_____

_____

_____

_____

3. How did you or how will you address the conflict?

EXERCISE TO REDUCE STRESS IN THE BODY

Spring is in full bloom, and we're growing in all directions! This is a beautiful process, but it does come with some growing pains. Let's alleviate them with this stretching sequence to reduce stress in your body.

Stand up straight with your feet shoulder width apart and your hands by your sides. Take a deep breath. Correct any slouching, and breathe again. Now reach toward your toes to the best of your ability (but don't overexert your-self!). Pull yourself upright again, and sit on the floor.

Stretch your legs straight out in front of you. Take a deep breath, and reach toward your toes, keeping your back as straight as you can. It's okay if your hands don't come close to your toes—you will still feel the stretch.

Release yourself from the stretch and lie back flat on the ground. Stretch your arms out so your body resembles a cross and take a breath. Bring your hands to your stomach and take another deep breath.

This sequence can be done at the pace of your choosing, but make sure you take enough time to breathe deeply and feel each stretch. Use the sequence as an opportunity to check in with your body and identify which places are holding more stress than others.

Reflect on your growth this season:

1. What has changed in your well-being since the spring began?

_____

_____

_____

_____

_____

_____

_____

_____

_____

_____

_____

2. Describe the state of your leaves, trunk, and roots.

_____

_____

_____

_____

_____

_____

_____

_____

_____

_____

_____

3. Do you feel energized? If not, what can be done now to prepare for improved growth in the next season?

_____

_____

_____

_____

_____

_____

_____

_____

_____

_____

_____

4. What is the most valuable lesson you learned this spring?

_____

_____

_____

_____

_____

_____

_____

_____

_____

_____

_____

_____

5. What brought you the most joy this spring?

_____

_____

_____

_____

_____

_____

_____

_____

_____

_____

_____

_____

6. What accomplishment of the spring are you most proud of?

_____

_____

_____

_____

_____

_____

_____

_____

_____

_____

_____

YEAR'S END

You have journaled your way through four seasons of growth! How does it feel?

Notice and appreciate the ways in which you have expanded your roots, strengthened your trunk, and grown bright green leaves. Now that we have pages of entries filled with reflections, thoughts, ideas, intentions, and experiences, we have a resource that is both an invaluable asset and a powerful tool. Hold on to this resource and review it in seasons to come. Write new entries reflecting on your initial responses; consider what has changed in your life and what has stayed the same. Decades of journaling have given me a stack of books to review, and I use them to reflect on how much I've grown, to find patterns in my choices and obstacles, and to entertain myself for hours. My priorities, thoughts, likes, and dislikes have all shifted over the years.

Thirty-six-year-old me gets a kick out of reading what nineteen-year-old Marcus was writing about! My reflection on these entries changes every year when I review them. Twenty-two-year-old me still felt the pain of my nineteen-year-old adolescent experiences, while twenty-six-year-old me felt proud of what I had overcome. I've improved my understanding of myself by strengthening a connection to my past, monitoring my growth, and clarifying my vision for the future.

Regardless of whether this is your first journal or your sixth, I encourage you to continue journaling going forward. Our journal is there to celebrate us in times of joy and support us in moments of adversity. It doesn't judge; it simply listens and gives us a place to be completely honest about our experiences.

Remember that the prompts, activities, and exercises are not limited to the section they are a part of. Now that you've tried them, do them again at different parts of the year and in different places (adjusting for the season, if need be). The subtle differences in time and space could have a profound impact on what you share. Compare them to your initial responses and see what you learn.

Now let's revisit the prompts of the introduction:

1. Who are you?

_____

_____

_____

_____

_____

_____

_____

_____

_____

_____

2. What is the current state of your well-being (your mental health, physical fitness, and spiritual awareness)?

_____

_____

_____

_____

_____

_____

_____

_____

_____

3. What are your goals for the coming year?

_____

_____

_____

_____

_____

_____

_____

_____

_____

_____

_____

_____

_____

4. Why is your well-being important?

_____

_____

_____

_____

_____

_____

_____

_____

_____

_____

_____

_____

5. What is your current routine for managing your well-being?

_____

_____

_____

_____

_____

_____

_____

_____

_____

_____

_____

_____

6. What does growth mean to you?

_____

_____

_____

_____

_____

_____

_____

_____

_____

_____

_____

_____

7. Describe your growth over the past year.

8. Do you feel stunted in your growth or supported?

9. What would you like your growth to look like a year from now?

_____

_____

_____

_____

_____

_____

_____

_____

_____

_____

Look at your initial responses from a year ago and your recent responses.

1. Have any of your responses changed? How so?

_____

_____

_____

_____

_____

_____

_____

_____

_____

2. What have you learned since your initial responses?

_____

_____

_____

_____

_____

_____

_____

_____

_____

_____

3. Have you noticed any patterns in your behavior, mood, or thought process?

_____

_____

_____

_____

_____

_____

_____

_____

_____

_____

4. Where have you made progress?

_____

_____

_____

_____

_____

_____

_____

_____

_____

_____

5. Did any of your responses (either from a year ago or recently) surprise you?

_____

_____

_____

_____

_____

_____

_____

_____

_____

_____

_____

6. Has journaling through the year affected your responses? How so?

_____

_____

_____

_____

_____

_____

_____

_____

_____

_____

_____

7. Have your interactions with your community and environment changed as a result of journaling? How so?

_____

_____

_____

_____

_____

_____

_____

_____

_____

_____

Finally, remember your journal is not exclusively a tool for *your* well-being. The more peace, balance, and harmony you have in your mind, body, and spirit, the better you can contribute to the well-being of those around you and the places you share with them. By taking care of yourself, you're taking care of others.

Congratulations on journaling through the year, and here's to the entries to come!

May your pen and paper meet at the crossroads of your thoughts and steer you in the direction of growth and prosperity.

ACKNOWLEDGMENTS

In the forest of our community, each tree has a purpose, and I find myself thinking about the "trees" in my life as I wrap up this book.

The forest of my community experienced two major changes as I worked on this manuscript: the loss of the oldest tree and the sprouting of its youngest.

I held the hand of my grandmother, Pearl Mason (August 13, 1927–April 23, 2023), as she departed from this lifetime. I thank her for her love and friendship, and I will always remember her resilience, kindness, and wit. I hope my life honors the legacy she left behind. Thank you, Pearl, for the fruits of wisdom you shared with me.

Months after losing Pearl, I caught my son, Imriel, as he transitioned from womb to world. Caring for hundreds of plants calls for kindness, patience, and positivity; caring for a baby calls upon all these qualities and more. I thank my son for teaching me how to be a better nurturer and for the joy he has brought to my life. In what was one of the more difficult years I have experienced, his heartwarming smile and bright spirit reminded me why I persevere. The loss of one tree calls for a new one to create balance in the forest, and I know my grandmother smiles upon him.

I thank my mother, Cheradin, for encouraging me to focus on growing strong roots. We have weathered serious challenges, individually and together, but she has stood unwavering against every tidal wave and storm. What a force you are, Mother! Despite any obstacle you face, you are always giving to others; you continue to be the most selfless person I know. I am grateful for you. Your grandson is fortunate to have you as an example in his life as I had in Pearl.

Finally, I thank my wife, Dana, for pushing me to flower. She made me believe I had something to share with the world and helped me do so. This year she showed me beauty and strength with her dedication to growing, birthing, and caring for our child. I will never forget how she walked out of the birthing center hours after delivery, as if she had not just performed life's miracle, and seamlessly fell into motherhood. Your love has been my life's greatest fertilizer. I love you.

ABOUT THE AUTHOR

MARCUS BRIDGEWATER is a creator, educator, motivational speaker, and plant enthusiast. He is the personality behind Garden Marcus on social media, which demonstrates that a positive, knowledgeable approach to nurturing plants also helps us grow as people. He is the founder and CEO of Choice Forward, a company that offers life-coaching, well-being workshops, and retreats, and he is the author of *How to Grow: Nurture Your Garden, Nurture Yourself.*